Experiences
of
Tao Te Ching

Collection
of
Poems

Includes
Interactive Journal

RW Hunker Jr

Experiences of Tao Te Ching
Copyright © 2023 by RW Hunker Jr

Published by
RW Hunker Jr
Carbondale, Colorado

ISBN: 979-8-218-21335-0

Cover Aerial Photo
RW Hunker Jr

Cover Design
RW Hunker Jr & Alyssa Ohnmacht

Edited by
Kristin Carlson

Light of the Moon, Inc.
Partnering with independent authors since 2009
Book Design/Production/Consulting
Carbondale, Colorado • www.lightofthemooninc.com

Gratitude

Experiences of Tao Te Ching
Collection of Poems

Introduction

I am a student of
Tao Te Ching, Dao De Jing
Tao-Te, Tao

take your choice of words, spellings
understand true *Tao*
is wordless, speechless

these poems are paradoxical
describing my experiences with *Tao*
with words that cannot
capture its essence

I discovered the written *Tao Te Ching* in 2010
when I was sixty-one years old
the more I read, the more I realized
I had experienced the living spirit of *Tao Te Ching*
many times, through an enduring relationship with *Nature*
which began when I was a child playing in the snow

these poems are not a translation of *Tao Te Ching*
rather, they express my experiences
interpretations and impressions
of the eighty-one verses

there is purposeful repetition in these poems
as there is in the verses of *Tao Te Ching*

silently, or adventurously out loud, read the poems
visualize each stanza
I invite you to reflect
on your own life by the *attribute* of each verse
feel free to journal or sketch
your experiences or visions
on the blank page adjacent to each verse

my soul is forever grateful
for the texts and experiences that inspired this book
my hope is that *Tao Te Ching*
will enhance your life with *Nature*
as it has enhanced mine

Tao Experience Journal

I invite you
to write or sketch
your own experiences or visions
for each of the *attributes*
that are presented
in these *poems*

do you have a favorite *Tao Te Ching* author?
read the corresponding verse
of their book
along with mine
and then journal
your thoughts
on the blank page

are you new to *Tao?*
I recommend you explore
Tao Te Ching writings
from authors I mention
in the *Afterword* portion of this book

go ahead
express your *true nature*
with *Tao*

The 81 *Attributes* of *Tao Te Ching*　　RW Hunker Jr

1	Mystery	42	Creation
2	Duality	43	Without Attachment
3	Empty	44	Contentment
4	Infinite	45	Silence
5	Impartial	46	Satisfaction
6	Essence	47	Light
7	Eternal	48	Wu-Wei
8	Water Course	49	Trust
9	Moderation	50	Immortality
10	Meditation	51	Growth
11	Inner Space	52	Existence
12	Sensory	53	Unhurried
13	Selflessness	54	Still Point
14	Formless	55	Harmony
15	Patience	56	Attention
16	Source	57	Noninterference
17	Leadership	58	Freedom
18	Compassion	59	Allow
19	Wisdom	60	Present Moment
20	Awe	61	Humility
21	Awareness	62	Open
22	Flexibility	63	Effort
23	Words	64	Carefree Wandering
24	Destiny	65	Naturally
25	Tao	66	Stream
26	Calm	67	Awake
27	Path	68	Be at Ease
28	Te	69	Bend
29	Balance	70	Way
30	Without Force	71	Receptive
31	Without Weapons	72	Release
32	As Is	73	Natural Responses
33	Holistic	74	Change
34	Flow	75	Detachment
35	Unseen	76	Softly
36	Let Go	77	Adaptability
37	Simplicity	78	Yield
38	Natural Order	79	Acceptance
39	Oneness	80	Peaceful
40	Cycles	81	Paradox
41	Time		

Tao is the way of *Nature*
Te is Humanity in harmony with the flow of *Tao*
Ching is a book

v1
Mystery

look up
clear, dark night sky
infinite points of light

above
pure experience
without words
without naming
without knowing

emptiness
full of life
here & everywhere

nature
opens
unknown paths

be in
wonder

Mystery

v2
Duality

first breath
birth of consciousness
journey into life

eyes
wide open
senses alert

last breath
death of consciousness
journey beyond life

eyes
closed
senses calm

universal life
endings
lead to
beginnings

wholeness
balance
peace

Duality

v3
Empty

sit
in silence

breathe in
calm

breathe out
noisy thoughts

begin
mantra

transcend
to *getting in the gap*
the space between thoughts

be *in the gap*
return *to the gap*
of a quiet mind

emptiness
contains
every possibility

Empty

v4
Infinite

mi amore

my love for you
cannot be contained
by this life
this fullest of passions
will go on forevermore

thank you for being
who you are
who you were
who you will be

as our souls
evolve
holistically
together

as we
hike mountains
paddle still water
swim ocean waves
feel spiritual mindfulness

we become
fluid
waves of love
and contentment

aloha

Infinite

v5
Impartial

soar
on the soft glow
of sunshine beams
breaking through
smooth stratus clouds

ride the sky
with the ultimate freedom of movement
where all
physical, emotional, spiritual
dimensions converge

view
up, down, across
all around
nature

earth
beauty
everywhere

without
prejudices, opinions
of right/wrong
good/bad

nature is impartial
be *nature*

fly
here, now
on earth
with empathy
for all life

Impartial

v6
Essence

walk through
an aspen grove of trees
shimmering with
yellow-orange leaves

breathe in
a deep, blue sky
crisp, cool air

fresh snow dusts the peaks
ahh
visual emotional delight
one with *mother*

changing seasons
move within us
expressing our souls

creation
the essence
of existence

alive

Essence

v7
Eternal

feel
unseen energies
move through your body

assume a
standing posture
breathe in new life force
breathe out the past

release tension
cleanse the body and
clear the mind

gather energy from the earth
gather energy from the cosmos

carry *chi*
expand & consolidate
move stillness
open to the unknown

receive from the *etheric* realm
hands to heart
love
forgiveness
gratitude

energy surrounds you
open and unified
bring in and send out
peace
stillness
calm

fulfillment

Eternal

Water Course

solid
liquid
vapor

water
travels by
precipitation
metamorphism
sublimation

engage snow
slide with skis
engage ice
slide with skates

engage water
drink
bathe
soak
swim
dive
paddle
sail

engage air
breathe in deeply
breathe out gently
fly
electric powered *ultralight* aircraft
soar the sky by sailplane

be
fluid dynamics
nourished
cleansed

oppose nothing
flow through everything

enjoy another drink of water

Water Course

v9
Moderation

too much
buy buy buy
possessions
egos

too many
fossil fuel products
human beings on
earth

more more more
overdoing anything
breeds losses
for all

nature knows
when
enough is enough

excess
is moderated by
balancing life events

can we let go
before
enough is too much?

Moderation

v10
Meditation

three small split logs
connect vertically
create a *tipi*
in the
adobe kiva fireplace

dark, quiet space
bring on light
spark the fire

yellow blue white
flames
dance high & higher
mesmerize your gaze

blazing flames
absorb your thoughts
clear your mind
create an empty space

the fire-engulfed *tipi*
collapses
into itself
becoming
glowing embers

your pulsating focus
like a healthy heartbeat
softens in the calm emptiness

coals to ash
light to darkness
nowhere & everywhere

it's time to sleep

Meditation

v11
Inner Space

night in a
desert landscape on
earth

overcast
dark without starlight
dark everywhere
not even a glimmer of artificial light

calm air
void of sound
nothing moving

dark & still
empty
silence
in & out

eyes open
dark and sightless
eyes closed
dark & sightless

neither hot nor cold
without smell or touch
can you sense your
inner breath?

rest in the womb
of *mother nature*
feel her lungs
expand & contract
content with
your inner space

Inner Space

v12
Sensory

they mate forever
walking
swimming
flying

devoted pairs
of canadian geese
take turns caring
always, one stands vigil
while the other grazes

do geese ever overindulge?
or is sensory overload
only a human condition

when you observe & feel
colors, sounds, flavors
are you consumed
by illusions?

pleasure & pain come & go
release all desire for more
free the slave from addiction

aware of the world
be in it
while not being in it

relax
go deeply within
care for your soul
cultivate an inner view
beyond the reality of the senses

walk, swim, fly
be in harmony
with the family
of all living things

Sensory

v13
Selflessness

nature
does not
live
for itself

sun
provides
warmth
water
gives
life

give
without expectation
of success or failure

be as *nature*
beyond ego body
trust your
inner nature

see
all things as part of us
serve, cherish, love
the universe

Selflessness

v14
Formless

listen
bach piano
goldberg variations

imagine a formless
sound of the
cosmos

it can not
be seen, touched
formless

before birth
after death
formless

live
aware
of the shapeless
source of spirit
spark of creation

our hearts
connected to
a natural, formless one

if death
is not
the end
would we change
how we live today?

Formless

v15
Patience

black & white
cat
crouched, silent, focused
waiting & waiting

we too can be
watchful
unmoving
aware of
our surroundings
outside & in

relaxed stillness
yields
unhurried waiting

open
observe
all things
settle your muddy waters
for a clear view

our patient focus
flows to
thoughtful
harmonious actions

Patience

v16
Source

where
did we
come from?

universe
stars
original *nature*

circular
cyclical
experiences

beginnings
endings
beginnings
renewals

still now
empty
all thoughts
all activities
cease

from the
source of tranquility
arises
divine love

inner peaceful heart
you
have returned home
to me

Source

v17
Leadership

teach
being invisible
trust
others

listen
carefully
encourage choices
let decisions be

learn
grow
share
lean into
self-sufficiency
and cooperation

stretch
visions, words, actions
embrace
flexibility

how we live
leads to what life brings
flying
serving
loving

Leadership

v18
Compassion

sun
moon
earth
harmony

human beings
tribes
families
harmony

why not?

live within the
tides & seasons
of *nature*

see
all living things
as spiritual souls
deserving respect

act
from the heart
with kindness
and altruism

express
compassion
for the
suffering
in
all of us

beyond
thoughts and words
can compassion be
our core identity?

Compassion

v19
Wisdom

field of
tall grass
sways
back & forth
with the
breeze

simple
plain
holistic
cooperative
movements

blow away
selfish desires
intellectual striving
attachment to experiences

cultivate
true natural
generosity

feel the
tall grass
wave within
your
heart & belly

Wisdom

v20
Awe

altitude
high above ground
airspeed slow, slower
wingspan nearly touching
the southwest-facing cliff
of *west beckwith* mountain

turn, circle to the north
around the mountain peak
sunlight
streams through the higher broken cloud layer
illuminating
the summit

bask in the
presence of
all things
seen/unseen

rotate to the
clear horizon
of the western sky
with infinite joy

ephemeral awe
inspired by
stellar source

Awe

v21
Awareness

breathe
in/out
feel/hear
life force

trust
intuition
know who you are
when connected
to source

observe
outside yourself
without judgment

sky, sun, clouds
mountains, rivers
nature
from afar
everything sings
in harmony
nothing needs to be changed

view your personal environment
up close
peer into the mysterious
simplicity
of all creation

now, do you really
need to change what you see
or can you let it be?

Awareness

v22
Flexibility

unsettled weather
rattles my mind
my life

pliant
plants, tree branches
bend, absorb, shed
winter snowfall

nature
adapts
changes
breathes anew

be as *nature*

all things pass
our thoughts
the exterior world

stretch your body
practice *qigong*
empty
your mind
feel the catharsis

be flexible
you are
alive, whole
evolving

Flexibility

v23
Words

you will always be with me
i will always be with you

thank you for all we shared
our journey together

my loss
your loss

oh, oh
life without you

the natural cycle
storm to calm
in time
rebirth

i will open to
new experiences
create
give
receive
love
again

let go of now's
thoughts & words
welcome
unknown sunlit possibilities

Words

v24
Destiny

born
pisces

under a sky
of descending
soft snowflakes

now the
spring snowpack
melts
flows to
streams, rivers, oceans

water
evaporates
becoming clouds
that saturate the
greater atmosphere

snow
falls from the sky
and the fluid cycle
repeats again & again

i, too, move
with fluid ease

on skis
in a kayak
or flying with wings
all
become extensions
of my physical body

innate
life choices
coexist
with *nature's*
fluid dynamics

thank you for the flow
of *tao te* blessings

Destiny

v25
Tao

mysterious
creation of all things
visible & invisible
great & small
near & far
universal

empty & full
without
words, categories, judgments

tao
manifests
timeless energy transfer
birth, death, rebirth

tao
within you & me

i feel *tao*
mountain climbing
desert hiking
floating on a gentle river
standing still

i connect with *tao*
through *nature's* seasons
silent gratitude meditation
awareness beyond myself

humanity has lost its soul
to digital-screens and pop culture

may *tao* simplicity
rebirth us into
sunny days
and starry nights

Tao

v26
Calm

when our minds churn
stirring up turbulence
inciting confusion
inside & out
look to *nature*

let the soft blanket
of a silent overcast sky
and the still surface
of water in the lake
offer a moment of calm

our minds serene
unmoved by
attractions/distractions
of life
can we choose
serenity over turbulence?

tranquil
as a tree
with deep roots
and flexible branches
we can bend in the wind
of a storm

centered on
silent mantras
grounded by
quiet meditation

we can be
nature's colorful
sunrise/sunset
over a calm sea

Calm

v27
Path

journey with *nature*
like flowing water
leave no signs of passage

one
with the river
flowing from eddies
through rapids
to eddies

a kayak
an extension of body
moving in harmony
with water

let
nature
our teacher
refine us
awaken
our energy & spirit
welcome
evolving understanding
give & receive
with spontaneity

your magical path
is the mystery
within your heart

Path

v28
Te

we embody
te
the human communion
wtih *tao*

our internal virtues
and loving qualities of being
express connection
to all things *tao*

when we embrace
tao
we can
balance
yin/yang
female/male
energies
create harmony
through humble, silent
awareness

draw energy inward
through meditation
surrender
in quiet stillness
to a comfy nap
with a purring cat

release energy outward
walk briskly/walk slowly
listen/talk
interact/create

let *true nature*
reveal itself
through us
simple, graceful
playful, childlike
brilliant
loving

Te

v29
Balance

humans
control earth
destroy earth

we
overpopulate
over consume
drown in excesses

humans are
out of balance with
our *mother*
nature

climate change
fires, floods, hurricanes
hot hot hot
viruses

nature
restores
balance
with or without
us

sun rises
sun sets
seasons rotate
spring, summer, autumn, winter

imagine
being in balance
with our planet
our home

Balance

v30
Without Force

force/counterforce
danger
struggle breeds stress
induces loss
on both sides

refuse force
open to
conflict-free existence
inside/outside

effortless effort
thoughts, words, actions
let go of
the battle

let us meet on a
level field, in the spring grass
beyond
right/wrong

listen
forgiveness
is the connecting music of
our spheres

plant
flowers
vegetable gardens
nurture the delicate growth
of your peaceful spirit
the tender shoots of sharing

Without Force

v31
Without Weapons

hate, fear, violence
funerals
weapons

words
spoken/written
ugly
weapons

social media platforms
culture clashes
weapons

political
misinformation/disinformation
weapons

family, friends
personal interactions
physical/verbal/emotional/psychological
weapons

disarm
all weapons

read & recite
love
poems

invite
the brilliant whole light
of the full moon
to shine through our souls

Without Weapons

v32
As Is

view
experience
your environment
without
names or categorizations of
things

ride
ocean
waves
balance
with the flow

let
your senses
see, hear, breathe
naturally
without
judgment

free
from your control
diet, body, mind
family, children
other people
future outcomes

feel
your energetic body
in movement & stillness
through the practice of *qigong*

acknowledge
all
as is

As Is

v33
Holistic

observe from space
beautiful earth
white clouds
blue oceans
red/green lands
holistic sphere

view
from the center of
being
know thyself and others as
one

everything
effects
everything else
the whole is greater than
the diversity of its individual parts

cultivate a whole soul
connect
mind, body, spirit

live
balanced, enlightened
and open hearted

all of us
looking, walking, talking, listening, loving
and spinning
around & around & around
in a holistic creation

Holistic

v34
Flow

fluid dynamics
subtle & powerful
moves invisibly
within creation's entirety

stunning flower petal
stellar snowflake
golden aspen leaf
sparkling dew drop
blink of the eye
momentary thought

babbling brooks
merging streams
cascading waterfalls
small rivers
larger rivers
vast oceans
and the unknown

insects, birds
fish, mammals
friends, strangers
lovers, children
yourself

invisible/visible *tao*
nourishes everything
within infinity

flow with *tao*
feel the current
slip
around, over, under
obstacles

relax
life with *tao*
can be
smooth
satisfying
joyous

Flow

v35
Unseen

clear
bluebird
sky

cold, dense air
southwest, tailwind breeze

approaching the southwest ridge
of *marcillina* mountain at
10,400 feet *mean sea level*

envision
the unseen air flow
up & over the ridge
smooth on the windward side
turbulent on the leeward side

fly
turn south
avoid the rough air

trust the path
of invisible *tao*
if offers
safety, wonder
formless pleasure

being
humble, quiet
joy & happiness
transcend
human physical form
a natural bliss
invisible as air

Unseen

v36
Let Go

of
desire, want
clinging thoughts
hyper ego
battleground mind
muddy waters

imagine a mind
as clear water
freely flowing
anonymously
giving
from a soft soul

natural cycle
returns then receives
abundantly
what you give
gratefully

empty
your cup
of past actions
memories

refill your cup
with a spacious mind
and as-is awareness
quench the thirst of want
with true nourishment

know
you are loved

Let Go

v37
Simplicity

organisms, systems
appear complex
evolve toward
greater levels
of complexity

nature
appears
just as it is
simple

we tend to
break apart
the whole
and analyze
the parts

nature
without effort
transforms
itself
simply

the unnecessary complexity of our
thoughts, creations, and possessions
clutters life's peaceful
harmonious
clarity

tao is
the architect
of simplicity

Simplicity

v38
Natural Order

snowing
white, soft, refreshing
each snow crystal of connected branches
revolves around a whole center

each crystal joins other crystals
creating layered snowpacks
of cohesive/cohesionless ice grains

diversified snowpacks
transform energy
into atmospheric vapor
as snow melts to water
captured by streams

water returns
to the cloud source
and falls again
to blanket the earth
with abundance

snow acts without
sense of self or intention
snow gives without
conditions or expectations

experience life & death
with *effortless effort*
be a stellar snow crystal
fluid as *true nature*

Natural Order

v39
Oneness

beginning
of all things
one
everlasting

core
of everything
cosmos
particles
oneness

clear skies
natural earth landscapes
clarity of mind
tranquility of heart

oneness
divine essence
zestful energy
fertile valleys

we are sky/earth spirits
expressions of love
all parts of a whole

cultivate
harmonize
sing into being
a global environment
of humility

or suffer
the consequences
of species extinction
including us

Oneness

v40
Cycles

death
comes
naturally
or
unbidden

aspen
leaves
die
every autumn

aspen
leaves
bud
anew
every spring

all natural
living things
return to the
mysterious origin

cycles
bear us
from nonbeing
to being
to nonbeing

yield
surrender
ego fear

trust
true spirit
to ignite
a flame
within the unknown

Cycles

v41
Time

past
present
future
interactive

thoughts
memories
visions
realities
illusions

time
without form
beyond boundaries
nameless

time is
an illusion

oh, humor
the paradox of
life & time

may our simple path
invite & accept
the wide-open vistas
of infinity

Time

v42
Creation

essence
existence
meaning
purpose

blank white canvas board
rainbow-colored paints
broad wavy brush strokes
red-orange sunset sky
blue ocean water
white-sand beach

happy birthday
mi amore
celebrate the
birth
of all things

write, sketch, paint
design, compose
photograph, film
record sound & voice
build
plant

nothing
becomes
everything
carry *yin*
embrace *yang*
blend dances
breathe harmony

give away
art
receive
abundance
in return

Creation

v43
Without Attachment

soft water
flows over & around
hard marble rock slabs
in the river bed

enter
the ocean
swim with
smooth flowing strokes

float
flexible
without attachment
to outcomes

act
without conscious effort
without controlled resistance

feel the natural rhythms
of unconditional love
within families, relationships, all energies

nature's
ongoing change
means nothing needs to be changed
relax

fly free
empty/full
silent/aware
thankful for
ordinary, everyday miracles

Without Attachment

v44
Contentment

fulfillment
treasures
within/without
exactly
as is

gather
no more
let go of the
chase

no worries
of being judged
no expectations
of producing products

listen, integrate
a dreamy andante
debussy piano sonata
into your soul

focus, embrace a
clear early evening sky
with a crescent moon rising
into still air

silently rejoice
appreciate
all the gifts
of life

by an inspired
gratitude
of
contentment

Contentment

v45
Silence

noisy world
noisy mind
overwhelming
noise

silence
empty/full
one with the
boundless source

stand still outside
as gentle snow
falls vertically
all around

silence
the space
between
thoughts, musical notes
the gaps of a
quiet mind

tranquil inner vision
guides
observation of
worldly *true nature*

communicate
using few words
convey peace
with silence

Silence

v46
Satisfaction

rolling stones
can't get
no satisfaction
from pop culture

a calm pond ripples
with light paddle strokes
as a kayak glides
on smooth water

chirping birds perch on
marshy cat tails
loons dive
disappearing, resurfacing

geese pairs
fly low, skimming the water
a solo bald eagle
circles
high above

floating still
soul bonded to *nature's* stage
satisfied, grateful, happy

Satisfaction

v47
Light

live
without seeking
the outside strobe lights
of urban pollution

all hearts beat
in rhythm
with every
flower, tree
earthly life and
heavenly sphere

open
hearts to
inner light

journey within
to follow the way of
untamed beauty
vision, core energy

be
spiritual light
in cosmic awareness

choose to
shine bright
connect to source
travel
without leaving home

Light

v48
Wu-Wei

reddish moon
rises on the eastern horizon
blue moon
arches above
light-grey moon
sets in the western sky
effortless effort
wu-wei

aspen trees
bud in spring
sprout summer-green leaves
burst with autumn-yellow glory
in winter
bare branches sleep
effortless effort
wu-wei

as *nature* goes
so we go
birth, growth, rebirth
a paradox of
self-conscious intention
and knowledge

desire less
discard complexity
decrease accumulation
act without attachment

ease into simple living
join the natural cycle of ebb & flow
let go
everything fulfilled
effortless effort
wu-wei

breathe in deeply
breathe out completely
be a flower, cloud, sunset, star
a generative source
wu-wei

Wu-Wei

v49
Trust

new neighbors
sport dreadlocks & tattoos
chain-smoke cigarettes

unaware
of their new surroundings & adjacent neighbors
they are loud, selfish
different
they have nothing in common
with us

really?

stop judging
open to generous
peaceful thoughts
they are us
namaste

welcome
be kind
radiate trust
all around
it returns

trust love
thrive together
nurture relationships
harmony soars
tears flow

compassion
community
connection
hello

Trust

v50
Immortality

fog rolls in
presence
fog dissipates
absence
regenerative cycle
of immortality

misty clouds
have no fear of *absence*
nine out of ten of us
are afraid
of physical *absence*
death

behold
nature
life passes to death
returns, reborn
nothing ends with death
including us

physical bodies decay, depart
spiritual beings transcend
open to the unknown

live now
without
illusions, resistance
suffering, fear

nourish *chi*
with a healthy lifestyle of
food, thoughts, emotions, relationships
relaxed, inclusive, loving

death
witness ending without ending

Immortality

v51
Growth

dawn of
consciousness
birth
of physical form
inherent power
natural life force

freedom to grow
nurtured & protected
by natural unseen virtue

create
without possessing
give
without expectations

honor
the mysterious source
with humility
without forethought

effortless, spontaneous actions
inspire
joyful hearts

alive now
evolve as the flow of
streams, rivers, oceans
the atmosphere & cosmos

grow beyond
a physical body
plant love
harvest & share
the flowers & fruit

Growth

v52
Existence

we
children of *mother*
spirit & earth

journey
from origin
from home

emerge in
worldly activities
senses, thoughts
passions, distractions

go within
speechless, silent
stillness
of a clear mind

see things
as they are
ephemeral
and everlasting

perceive
microscopic life
in illuminating snow crystals
interconnections
of all things
whole

sense radiant light
blossom with awareness
of the eternal spirit

your child self
returns to *mother*
the unseen source
of compassion

simply love

Existence

v53
Unhurried

fast, faster
technological advances
where are we going?

distractions everywhere
side paths
where is the way?

rich, richer
others impoverished
out of balance

mind clutter
disrupting
healthy *chi*

wake up
slow down
smell the earth
glide on water
open up
walk, listen, talk

birds sing
aspen leaves shimmer

two bald eagles sit together, side by side
on a high branch overlooking the river

a butterfly hovers
above a cluster
of bluebell flowers

may our pace
be unhurried
on the smooth pathway
of peace

Unhurried

v54
Still Point

deep roots
in our hearts
cultivate
flowers, fruit

our loving nature
within
visibly
spreads
inclusivity, prosperity, peace

feel the *still point*

in moments of whole awareness
where soul-source shines
authentic, simple, honest

in silent space
where every breath
in & out
pulsates
with interconnecting waves
of harmony

families
villages, nations
next generations
earth
all heavenly beings
revolve around the
still point between the next
sunrise & sunset

Still Point

v55
Harmony

piano notes
a, c#, e
blend into a
universal cord

soft newborn
flexible, open
powerful spirit
with a firm grip

perceive
a simple, natural way
to delight in discovery

release
stress, worry, fear
allow
nature's rhythm
to flow through you
unafraid

experience
fully
the present moment
selflessly

sing your song

Harmony

v56
Attention

inner knowledge
outer expression
hmm

listen inside
listen outside
share the intuitive journey

perception absent
of daily worldly
trauma

engage
locally
love
gently

hear birds chirp
in the early morning
ah
a hummingbird hovers
to drink from a sweet flower

thoughtful mind
still water
breezeless day

amazing present moment
simple splendor
of consciousness

Attention

v57
Noninterference

honesty
integrity
in the microcosm
and macrocosm
begin
within

institutions & government leaders
fail to lead us
into an evolving world
of personal & social
freedom

too many
restrictions, prohibitions
regulations
weapons
disordered relationships

overwhelm hope
of a harmonious society

visualize intentions
flexible & free of obsessive goals
control no one, nothing

acknowledge change
allow flow without force
live as *nature* lives
without interference
or cultural conditioning

desire nothing
act without attachment
embrace natural enrichment

we need no permission to be happy

Noninterference

v58
Freedom

unjust governments
control people
invade privacy
restrict individual choices

living
confused, lost
hopeless

inner perception
either fortunate or constrained
by the peaks & valleys
of being

be who you are

pause
take
slow deep breaths
listen
for quiet guidance
from your center

relinquish who you are to
inner wisdom
gut feelings
choice
freedom
loving flow

without judgment
of right or wrong
nature
acknowledges life
and welcomes everything

Freedom

v59
Allow

live an
example for
others to
follow

be
a leader for your
self
family
community
country
world

be
moderate
humble
honest
listen
to all
care for earth
and all her wonders

flow on the river of life
as clouds stream across the sky
sunlight shines visible, then hidden behind
majestic mountain peaks

connect to
great *mother's*
deep roots
and expansive skies
nothing is impossible

allow
anything to happen
nourish
spirit, soul
your enduring life force

Allow

v60
Present Moment

negative thoughts
overwhelm the
self

an open *tao* heart
evaporates
these
energies

be
without
categorizing
analyzing
or switching

dissolve the busy mind
simply observe a
moment of
nature
now

southwestern horizon
sky fully obscured
air beckons, this way

face the breeze
that cools the hot day

lightning approaches
thunder follows
distant rain showers
imminent
here

naked
nature sprinkles holy water
cleansing
body & soul

Present Moment

v61
Humility

ocean saltwater
gathers
all fresh water
from rivers
and precipitation
from the atmosphere

jump in
feel nurturing warmth
body & joint movement
fluid, soft, gentle
swim free

view underwater life
through a snorkel & mask
explore a novel world of
brightly colored
enchantment

ocean
powerful force
dynamic *yang* energy
yet, deep *yin* energy
humble in the womb
of *tao*

be as *yin* ocean
on land
humble in
interactions, relationships with
families, tribes, countries
and *nature*

leaders
are you
listening?

Humility

v62
Open

source of
creation
provides for
everyone
without
good or bad
judgments

enter
go inside *tao*
soften your
intuition
clear your
mind

forgive
past actions
yourself
others

you may experience
tao without knowing it
all of the sudden
you may be aware of
tao presence

reconnect your
spirit & soul
to a warm & peaceful journey
open to all
tao is home

Open

v63
Effort

challenging task
building an *experimental* airplane
from a kit full of parts
overwhelming uncertainty
of completion

one small piece at a time
focusing in the present with
attention to details
eases difficulty

simple components
join other components to
become a larger whole
a *homebuilt* airplane
comes together smoothly
with *effortless effort*

act with confidence
create without doing
without self-conscious
evaluation of
the external pressure
to complete the
bigger picture

now becomes now
becomes now
now the completed wing
takes flight
the dream
soars
in reality
with gratitude

Effort

v64
Carefree Wandering

begin
visualize a picture of
an adventure

do not force movement
be patient
without desire

choose free thoughts
and suffering vanishes
now, an infinite journey takes flight

what is your vision?
enter your dream world of
carefree wandering

listen to
john lennon's
imagine
life could be
peace & harmony

butterflies
join the dance

Carefree Wandering

v65
Naturally

here
the atmosphere above is clear & still
in the distance thunder rumbles

now
clouds
drift overhead
pass by, then disperse
the clear sky appears again

everything we
see, hear, touch, smell, feel
moves through us
like the passing clouds

our hearts intuitively
guide us
within the flowing
changes of life

keep things simple
thoughts, words, actions
as we touch
the warm embrace
of *tao*

Naturally

v66
Stream

floating through river rapids
as a spectator
brings memories alive
of a participant past

now, humble stories of elders
swirl around the paddles
of curious youthful guides

clear water
be clear water
muddy water
be muddy water
low & humble
as the riverbed
over which we float

continue
downstream
rest in an eddy
enter the flow
again

settle
again
in the calm pool
of serenity

Stream

v67
Awake

begin
travel
end
perceive
inside & outside
naturally

see
tiny blue dragonflies dancing
feel the
cool autumn breeze
hear the
steady gentle sound
of river water flowing

being present in the
here & now
reveals three treasures
of heart consciousness

loving compassion
patient simplicity
humble harmony

engage
all visible & invisible
energies
to radiate generosity

Awake

v68
Be at Ease

competition
creates must-win battles
outside & within

pause

open interaction invites
non-contention, cooperation
free of emotional striving

when we give up the fight
relinquish disagreements
dissolve anger & arrogance
we can move on with *effortless effort*

come to the stillness
that recharges our energy
renews our good humor
and reflects the peace of inner strength

smile, laugh
smell the sweet aroma
of gardenias

we can be at ease
all things pass

Be at Ease

v69
Bend

when rigid divisions
between uncompromising enemies
threaten to destroy us

time-out!

we can agree to disagree
saying no to fear or hate
shedding the armor of combat
we can soften our shells
and bend as we breathe

we can choose composure
open gently to compassion
even in gale-force winds
we can be flexible
as healthy palm trees

with energies balanced
and *hands to hearts*
we can begin to heal

Bend

v70
Way

tao
visible & invisible
simple in practice
how can
more of us experience it?

by entering the stillness of
our hearts & minds
by practicing *qigong*
centered in harmony

we can sense
how the natural world
mirrors art
aesthetic & blunt landscapes, horizons
show the way

we can be child-like
at any time in our life
uninhibited
by the vast emptiness
of a blank canvas
big as the sky

every open space
offers a fresh slate
where we can create art
reflect, and recreate our lives
with youthful wonder

by cleaning & exercising
our souls' homes often
we can be
in *tao* everywhere

Way

v71
Receptive

conditioned by
bubble environments
education, beliefs

we think
we know
everything

following our own advice
we become hollow echo chambers
filled with mental & physical dis-ease

tonight
outside in the dark
let's listen instead
to crickets singing

awake & receptive
to the music of diversity
mysteries will be revealed
to free minds

together
let's experience
the well being & innocence
of a healthy soul
senses attuned & attentive
to the here & now

Receptive

v72
Release

too often
we hold tight to troubled emotions
unsettled thoughts
trapping them inside

keep the lid on the pot
stir into a frenzy
and boil until hot

distrust institutions
fear the unknown
bow to the power
of religious doctrines
believe illusions

but today, we have a choice
to turn down the heat
and release the turbulent waters
of resentment before they overflow

this moment, right now
we can gather *nature's* awe
engage heart & spirit
forgive ourselves & others
radiate trust all around

a breeze stirs vibrant air
over the pond where
sunlight shimmers on
the surface
of still, deep waters

reflect in yourself
nature's humility

Release

v73
Natural Responses

trust *tao*
the invisible & unknown
be here now
no need to force change

listen
a light rain
soothes
the skylight window pane

look
dark clouds
break open
a sunlight beam appears
and a rainbow arches over
everyone
everywhere

be patient
silent yet responsive
with courage

experience
wu-wei
effortless effort
in every breath
along the *watercourse way*

Natural Responses

v74
Change

all things age
break down
pass
including
human bodies

our joints
stiff with arthritis
lose motion
ache with pain

organs
become sluggish
their failure causes death

pop-tech culture
persuades us to resist change
replace broken parts
endure surgery after surgery
become artificial intelligence

why?

because we fear death
we will try anything
to delay inevitable decay
and loss of self
all our earthy connections
and everything we have ever known

suffering
is the price we pay
for all our desperate efforts to escape change

bliss lies in awakening by
accepting living & dying
as the natural cycle of *tao*
to be celebrated in every grateful
peaceful, passing moment

Change

v75
Detachment

data and
numbers
9 8 7 6 5 4 3 2 1
0
our creation

nature
acts without
our calculus

when spiritually empty
we attempt to
control everything through
greed, judgment, fear
our souls suffer

when we detach
from ego expectations
pop culture entertainment
and following the numbers

we create space
to commune with *nature*
practice *qigong* and
we can drop deep into
wayne dyer's getting in the gap meditation

when we observe life
with a sense of humor
we have the energy
we need to fly free

Detachment

v76
Softly

remember *family*
in the present now

write poems on
grandmother's
99 year old, kidney-shaped desk

measure spaces with
grandfather's
antique, hinged, folding wooden ruler

play badminton with
father's
vintage, *wilson zephyr* racquet

grow garden snap peas like
mother's
eat them fresh from the pods

enjoy breakfast cereal from
sister's
handmade pottery bowl

honor *family*
thank you
for all you have given

talk today with
your
mother, father
brothers, sisters
children, grandchildren
best friend

i love you

Softly

v77
Adaptability

riverside hot springs
warm, mineral-water spa
jacuzzi hot tub
or a bath at home
soak
the body

each immersion in water
can ease
physical pain
and help wash away
mental obsessions

liquid life
sustains & surrounds us
as we move toward
body & mind
equilibrium

sip *green* tea
share from a
full cup
abundance
flows
through us
and beyond

Adaptability

v78
Yield

water
soft, adaptable, nurturing
powerful, destructive

the cycle of
fluid dynamics
draws water from oceans
to create rain, snow
to streams & rivers
and returns water
to the oceans again

too much
or not enough
water tells us
it's time
to wake-up

human hardness
has knocked us
out of balance
with earth's
flexible ways

overpopulation, excessive consumption
destruction of natural environments
selfishness with no regard
for diversity
within our species & beyond

who do we think we are?

with extinction on the horizon
dare we humble ourselves
to yield like water
and return to harmony
with all life on earth?

Yield

v79
Acceptance

disputes
unfair directives
negotiations
compromises
are stressful interactions

resentments with
family
friends
lovers
sow regrets
even estrangement

only forgiveness
of self & others
can heal
our humanity

only acceptance
of the past
and differing viewpoints
can free us
from sleepless nights

be generous
with no
expectation
of receiving

clear harmful thoughts
without judgment
accept
everything as it is

Acceptance

v80
Peaceful

all are welcome
in the wide open spaces
of paradise valley

living close with *nature*
we share common ground
warm homes & healthy plant-based food

our community
is like a bowl of mixed vegetables
full of different flavors
that enhance each other

here, we learn to
communicate & create music
without notation
with our bodies as instruments

here, we tell generational stories
sing, clap, dance
to express
the way we feel

clean from all addictive
prescription & recreational drugs
we can experience
the expanded consciousness
that connects us to *tao*

in the quiet dark of night
a peaceful sleep
welcomes our souls & spirits
with infinite gratitude

Peaceful

v81
Paradox

yule creek trail
is it a long hike
or a short trek?

each of us
creates our own
realities & illusions
empathetic or selfish

without words & concepts
we can experience *tao*
of landscapes, mountains, rivers, oceans
and drifting ephemeral clouds
that fill us with emptiness

absence brings forth *presence*
fluid energy becomes nothingness
formless consciousness
radiates regeneration

circular paths
return us
to one center
the source of
mysterious *tao*

Paradox

Afterword

I offer this book as a new expression of *Tao-Te Attributes*
inspired by my own experiences with the verses of *Tao Te Ching*
and rooted in appreciation for the teachers, mentors, and writers
who have come before me
thank you

William Martin
Solala Towler
Stephen Mitchell
Wayne Dyer
Derek Lin
Priya Hemenway
Karen Wyatt
Diane Dreher
Alan Watts
Rick Haltermann
Stanley Rosenthal
Matthew Cohen
David Hinton

I invite you to journey with *Tao Te Ching*
by reading books by these authors
and practicing *Qigong*

throughout the centuries
translations, interpretations, variations
of *Tao Te Ching*
have been written
verses which are expressed differently
retain common *Tao-Te Attributes*

as you discover & experience
your own *Tao* life
through the simplicity
of natural oneness

may *Wu-Wei* be with you

RW Hunhu S.
2023

Acknowledgements

I am deeply grateful to Lisa Wagner, *mi amore* along this journey of life, for her attentive commentary, with enduring and loving support. Thank you Gracie, our tuxedo cat, who is always by my side when I write.

Thank you Bill Martin for your inspiring *Tao Te Ching* writings and personal connection; Kristin Carlson, my editor, for opening my eyes to poetic clarity; Olivia Savard and Alyssa Ohnmacht of *Light of the Moon, Inc,* my publishing consultants, for being totally dedicated to the quality of this book.

Thank you, with tremendous appreciation, to everyone I have shared adventures in the snow, water, air, life ... and beyond.

About the Author

RW Hunker Jr

Connected with the written *Tao Te Ching* in 2010
began *Qigong* practice in 2015

Studied Buddhism in 1969
engaged with Transcendental Meditation (TM) in 1974

Earned a BA Psychology degree from
Western State College of Colorado in 1992

Authored *Tao Te Ching Card Readings* in 2016
and *Wellness Living Card Readings* in 2021

Wrote six *Creation Myth* poems, and two aviation books: *The Flights of Red Hill, volume 1, Flying Stories and Aerial Photography of Colorado's Elk Mountains* (2012); and *The Flights of Red Hill, volume 2, For Pilots Only, The Beginning* (2021).

Rob has experienced a lifetime of adventure and work with Nature in the snow, water, and air. He has forecasted snow avalanches and instructed whitewater kayaking and *ultralight* flying. His aerial photography library includes photographs and videos of the Colorado Elk Mountains from 2001-2022.

Rob's home is in the West Elk Mountains of Colorado
Contact him at: *rwhunker@gmail.com*

Gratitude

www.ingramcontent.com/pod-product-compliance
Lightning Source LLC
Chambersburg PA
CBHW051157120626
46547CB00012B/1102